S0-BDM-861

QUEEN CLEOPATRA

TOM STREISSGUTH

In Consultation with Martha Cosgrove,
M.A. and Reading Specialist

LERNER PUBLICATIONS COMPANY / MINNEAPOLIS

Martha Cosgrove has a master's degree from the University of Minnesota in secondary education, with an emphasis on developmental and remedial reading. She is licensed in 7–12 English and language arts, developmental reading, and remedial reading. She has had several works published, and she gives numerous state and national presentations in her areas of expertise.

Lerner Publications Company
A division of Lerner Publishing Group
241 First Avenue North
Minneapolis, Minnesota 55401 U.S.A.

Website address: www.lernerbooks.com

Library of Congress Cataloging-in-Publication Data

Streissguth, Thomas, 1958–
Queen Cleopatra / by Tom Streissguth.
p. cm. – (Just the facts biographies)
Includes bibliographical references and index.
ISBN-13: 978–0–8225–5979–5 (lib. bdg. : alk. paper)
ISBN-10: 0–8225–5979–X (lib. bdg. : alk. paper)
1. Cleopatra, Queen of Egypt, d. 30 B.C.–Juvenile literature. 2. Egypt–History–332–30 B.C.–Juvenile literature. 3. Queens–Egypt–Biography–Juvenile literature. I. Title.
DT92.7.S883 2007
932'.021092–dc22 [B] 2006024445

Manufactured in the United States of America
1 2 3 4 5 6 – DP – 12 11 10 09 08 07

Contents

CHAPTER 1 RULED BY STRANGERS

(Above) **Cleopatra was one of the wealthiest people in the ancient world.**

MORE THAN TWO THOUSAND YEARS AGO, in 41 B.C., the people of Tarsus were waiting near the Cydnus River. (Tarsus is a city in Asia Minor, part of what has since become Turkey.) The people watched as a huge boat called a barge sailed toward them. They were about to see someone special. Cleopatra VII, the wealthy queen of Egypt, was arriving. She was there to meet the Roman leader Mark Antony.

He was the most powerful man in the Roman world. She had obeyed his order to come to Tarsus.

Her barge had gold covering its front end. Its sails were purple. Musicians on the barge played flutes and harps. Silver oars powered the barge. Its crew included many women. They were dressed as figures from mythology.

The queen's boat anchored at the river's edge. Cleopatra waited on board. She ruled only Egypt. Antony controlled much of the area at the eastern end of the Mediterranean Sea. But his power didn't scare the proud queen. She decided to show Antony her independent spirit. He was waiting in Tarsus for the queen to come to him. More people rushed out of town to the riverbank. Cleopatra had come to Tarsus, as ordered. But she didn't leave her barge. Antony found himself alone, waiting for the queen.

Antony was proud too. But he was also good natured. He had important matters to settle with this queen. So he marched to her royal ship. He greeted her crew. Then he climbed aboard like any guest. There, he and Cleopatra struck a bargain to work together. Their bargain would change their lives. It would also shape the future of the Mediterranean world.

Roman Provinces
GAUL
TRANSALPINE GAUL
CISALPINE GAUL
ILLYRICUM
NEARER SPAIN
CORSICA
SARDINIA
SICILY
Rome
ITALY
Brundisium
Tarentum
MACEDONIA
Actium
ARCHAEA (GREECE)
BLACK SEA
BITHYNIA-PONTUS
ASIA MINOR
Ephesus
CILICIA
Cydnus R.
Tarsus
Antioch
CYPRUS
ARMENIA
Tigris R.
PARTHIAN EMPIRE
Euphrates R.
SYRIA
JUDAEA
ARABIA
AFRICA
NUMIDIA
MEDITERRANEAN SEA
Pelusium
Alexandria
CYRENE
EGYPTIAN KINGDOM
Nile R.
RED SEA
Cleopatra's Mediterranean World, 51 B.C.

ANCIENT EGYPT

Cleopatra's kingdom was in North Africa. The long Nile River flows north through Egypt toward the Mediterranean Sea. The waters feed a fertile valley. The valley supplied crops and other goods that made ancient Egypt rich. For thousands of years, Egypt's rulers, called pharaohs, had control here. They lived in great palaces. The Egyptian people worshipped their pharaohs like gods. The ancient Egyptians honored many different gods. Amon-Re was the most powerful of all the gods.

About three hundred years earlier, in 332 B.C., Alexander the Great of Macedonia took over Egypt. (Ancient Macedonia was a kingdom in what became northern Greece.) At only twenty-four, he had already conquered most of the eastern Mediterranean. The Egyptian religion fascinated Alexander. So, he made a holy journey to Siwah in western Egypt. In Siwah stood a temple to Amon-Re. Alexander made an offering to the god. In turn, the priests of Siwah named him as the son and living symbol of Amon-Re.

Before leaving Egypt, Alexander founded the port of Alexandria. The port sits on a narrow piece of land between the Mediterranean Sea and Lake

Alexander the Great

Mareotis. The small city attracted many settlers. People from Greece, Macedonia, and other parts of Alexander's empire came there to live.

After his trip to Siwah, Alexander conquered huge areas of the Middle East and Asia. But in 323 B.C., at the age of thirty-three, he suddenly died of a fever. His main generals–Antigonus, Seleucis, and Ptolemy–divided up the most valuable parts of Alexander's empire. Antigonus chose to rule Macedonia. Seleucis picked Syria and Persia (modern-day Iran). Ptolemy decided on Egypt.

Ptolemy brought Alexander's body to Alexandria and put it in a fancy tomb. He wanted to succeed Alexander. Placing Alexander's body in Egypt gave Ptolemy a better claim to the throne. Ptolemy also claimed he was related to Amon-Re. In 305 B.C., Ptolemy proclaimed himself Ptolemy I. He called himself pharaoh and divine ruler of Egypt. The Ptolemaic dynasty (family of rulers) had begun.

PTOLEMY I

Ptolemy I was not Egyptian. He was an outsider who spoke Greek. But he knew he had to act like an Egyptian pharaoh to win the Egyptian people's support. He held ceremonies in which people worshipped him. He directed artists to show him as a god in temple carvings and temple writings.

IT'S A FACT!

Ptolemy I and most of his successors never bothered to learn the ancient Egyptian language.

Alexandria grew as trade between Europe, Arabia, and India increased. Throughout the region, Greek was the language of trade. Merchants sold Egypt's grain. They showed off the kingdom's rare cloth, glass, jewelry, pottery, and metal goods. In Ptolemy's time, Alexandria was becoming the busiest and wealthiest port city in the Mediterranean region.

Ptolemy worked to bring Greek culture to Egypt. He built the Museum. In these buildings, Greek teachers educated wealthy Alexandrian children. He also set up the Library. It held thousands of Greek books on medicine, math, science, and poetry.

Who Is Who? What Is What?

Achillas (ah-KIL-uhs): an adviser to Cleopatra's brother, Ptolemy XIII

Alexander the Great: king of Macedonia, who later took over Greece, Egypt, Persia (modern Iran), Asia Minor (modern Turkey), and parts of India

Amon-Re: the most powerful god in the ancient Egyptian religion

Arsinoë IV (ahr-SIN-oh-ay the fourth): sister of Cleopatra

Auletes (oh-LEET-eez): Cleopatra's father, also known as Ptolemy XII *(left)*

Cleopatra VII: the last queen of Egypt

Julius Caesar: a Roman statesman and general. If he had not been murdered, he would likely have become the first emperor of Rome.

Mark Antony: a Roman general who sought control of the Roman Republic

Mediterranean Sea: a body of water between Europe and Africa. At the eastern end are the countries that make up the modern Middle East. At the western end are the countries that make up southern Europe and North Africa.

Nile River: the longest river in the world. It flows through eastern and northern Africa and empties into the Mediterranean Sea.

Octavia (ock-TAY-vee-uh): the sister of Octavius and the wife of Mark Antony

Octavius (ock-TAY-vee-uhn): the great nephew and heir of Julius Caesar. Octavius eventually fought Mark Antony for control of all Roman lands. After defeating Cleopatra and Antony, he became Augustus Caesar, the first Roman emperor.

Parthia: an ancient kingdom that roughly matches northeastern Iran

patrician: an upper-class Roman citizen

pharaoh (FAIR-oh): a ruler of ancient Egypt

Pothinus (puh-THY-nuhs): an adviser to Cleopatra's brother, Ptolemy XIII

Ptolemy (TAHL-uh-mee): the name of every king of Egypt within the family of rulers set up by Ptolemy I *(right)*

Roman Republic: the ancient Roman state that was ruled by an elected Senate

Theodotus (thee-UH-doh-tuhs): an adviser to Cleopatra's brother, Ptolemy XIII

The Library in Alexandria had an enormous collection of the works of ancient scholars.

The Library collected the knowledge and literature of the Mediterranean world up to that time.

For all its wealth, Alexandria was still an isolated city. Many Alexandrians were Greek settlers. They knew little of the rest of Egypt. They traded along the Mediterranean Sea. These Greek traders set up huge estates. Their laborers were poor native-born Egyptians who worked the land as slaves.

IT'S A FACT!

The Alexandria library didn't survive. Its many one-of-a-kind books were lost during fires and foreign takeovers.

In the Nile Valley, life hadn't changed much for thousands of years. Poor people lived in small villages. They farmed the land and traveled the Nile in boats. They carefully watched the yearly flooding of the Nile. This flooding began in late spring and went on for several months. In good years, the Nile watered fields and crops. The harvests were huge. In poor years, the fields were dry. Many Egyptians starved.

Later Ptolemies

The rulers who followed Ptolemy showed their strong link to him and Alexander. They kept the name of their dynasty's founder. By tradition, every king of Egypt called himself Ptolemy. All queens were named either Arsinoë, Berenice, or Cleopatra.

These rulers also continued Ptolemy I's religious practices. People worshipped them as

It's a Fact!

Arsinoë was the name of Ptolemy I's mother. And Berenice was one of his wives. Alexander the Great's sister was named Cleopatra, a name that means "glory of her father." Using these names over and over tied rulers to Ptolemy and Alexander.

Ptolemaic rulers had their portraits carved out of gems and coins. This third century B.C. portrait of Ptolemy II and his sister and wife, Arsinoë II, was carved out of a black stone called onyx.

ruler-gods. Artists showed them as gods on Egypt's huge monuments and temples. The ancient Egyptian religion said that a god could only marry another god. As a result, the Ptolemies married only within the Ptolemaic family. So, Ptolemy II, the son of Ptolemy I, married his sister Arsinoë II.

Ptolemy II's reign lasted for thirty-seven years, from 283 to 246 B.C. He made Egypt the strongest country in the eastern Mediterranean. Egyptian armies marched into nearby countries. The armies conquered many rich cities. Ptolemy III came next. He defeated several rivals to his family's rule. During his reign, Alexandria was the learning center of the Mediterranean world. It was home to top scholars, engineers, doctors, mathematicians, and artists.

After Ptolemy III's death, the Ptolemaic dynasty began to decline. The later Ptolemies were weak and greedy. They collected huge taxes. But they spent the money on themselves. They lived in

Guiding Light

Alexandria had a tall lighthouse *(below)*. It was called the Pharos ("lighthouse" in Greek). The Pharos was more than 500 feet (152 meters) tall. The lighthouse sat on an island near Alexandria's coast. A large torch of fire stood on top of the Pharos. It burned a bright beacon for ships at sea. Ships from all over the Mediterranean used the beacon to reach Alexandria safely.

luxury and threw big parties. At the same time, the rest of Egypt suffered through droughts and famines.

The eldest Ptolemaic son or daughter didn't inherit the kingdom by rule. The pharaohs played favorites. Children and relatives tried to win the king's favor. They hoped the pharaoh would name him or her the next pharaoh. But often these relatives plotted against and even murdered one another. These feuds sometimes spread into the streets of Alexandria and to the rest of Egypt. Groups loyal to one Ptolemy or another fought bloody civil wars. During these fights, the country lost the foreign lands it had conquered.

Among the groups taking over Egypt's former lands were the armies of the Roman Republic. This republic–a state ruled by a senate, not by a king–sat across the Mediterranean Sea from Egypt. Soon the Romans saw the weakness of the feuding Ptolemies. Roman leaders decided to take over the richest kingdom in the Mediterranean world–Egypt.

In Debt to the Romans

The feuding Ptolemies needed lots of money. They were still building palaces and monuments. They were still richly entertaining themselves. They also needed money to pay for their family feuds. In 88 B.C., Ptolemy X was plotting to defeat his rival Ptolemy IX. Ptolemy X borrowed a huge sum from a Roman moneylender. He was unable to pay back the money before he died. Ptolemy X left all of Egypt to the Romans in his will. The problem was he didn't actually have control of Egypt. In addition, his will wasn't legal under Roman law. The Roman moneylender couldn't collect. So the Romans allowed Ptolemy IX to rule in Egypt. But they forced the Egyptians to pay the debts of Ptolemy X.

After the death of Ptolemy IX in 81 B.C., Ptolemy XI came to the throne. His reign was short. Just a few weeks after becoming king, he murdered his stepmother. This act put the people in a rage.

Roman Numbers

The Romans had their own numbering system. Perhaps you've seen sporting events—such as Super Bowl XL—that use this system. For the Romans, letters stood for numbers. *I* stands for 1. *V* stands for 5. *X* stands for 10. *L* stands for 50. When a smaller number comes after a larger one, a user adds the total. So, in Cleopatra's case, V (5) plus II (2) equals 7. When a smaller number comes before a larger one, the user subtracts. So, in the Super Bowl XL example, X (10) is taken away from L (50) to make Super Bowl 40.

A giant mob chased him through the streets of Alexandria and killed him. His successor was Ptolemy XII. The Alexandrians nicknamed him Auletes (the Flute Player).

Auletes had six children by two wives. With his first wife, he had three daughters–Cleopatra VI, Berenice IV, and Cleopatra VII. Shortly after Cleopatra VII's birth, her mother died. Auletes remarried. With his second wife, he had two sons, Ptolemy XIII and Ptolemy XIV. They also had a daughter, Arsinoë IV. The members of Auletes' family would spend the rest of their lives plotting against one another. They hungered for the best prize of all. Each wanted to rule Egypt.

IT'S A FACT!

Alexandrians gave the Ptolemies nicknames. Some of them were not so nice. One family member was called Physcon (Fatty). Another was Lathyrus, or Chickpea.

CHAPTER 2 A VIOLENT WORLD

CLEOPATRA VII AND HER BROTHERS and sisters grew up in a palace complex along the shores of Alexandria. The complex was an amazing place. Beautiful stone columns lined the rooms. Artists decorated these rooms with statues and floor mosaics. Paintings lined the walls. The palace had wide porches that looked

(Above) **Cleopatra grew up surrounded by luxury and danger. This piece of art is from the 1800s.**

out over the city and the sea. The complex's surrounding gardens held sparkling fountains. The palace's treasury stored a fortune in gold, gems, and jewelry. Hundreds of servants took care of Cleopatra's father and his family. They had the best doctors and tutors (teachers). Skillful cooks made fabulous meals. And a small army of guards surrounded the family.

Growing Up Sneaky

Cleopatra VII received an outstanding education. She studied at home with tutors. But she also went to the Museum. She learned math, literature, art, music, medicine, and foreign languages.

Despite having guards, the palace complex wasn't safe. The scheming family members made the palace a dangerous place to live. As a young girl, Cleopatra found out that relatives had murdered many members of her family. Some had been poisoned.

It's a Fact!

As an adult, Cleopatra could speak Egyptian, Greek, Aramaic (a form of Greek), Hebrew, and Ethiopic. She also knew Latin, the language of the Romans.

Finding Cleopatra's Palace

About seventeen thousand years ago, in A.D. 335, a powerful earthquake struck Alexandria. Soon afterward, a huge wave crashed into the city. It flooded the shores of the eastern harbor. Many ancient homes and monuments were destroyed. Since that day, the area where Cleopatra lived has been under 20 feet (6 m) of water.

In June 1996, a French explorer named Franck Goddio set out to find Cleopatra's drowned palace. He and his team dove thousands of times in the ancient eastern harbor. The team found paved streets, statues, granite columns, and thousands of building fragments. They also found the remains of the ancient port.

Several years later, ancient Alexandria was opened to tourists. Visitors can see Cleopatra's palace by diving or by submarine. Modern Alexandria also set up a new Alexandrian library in the ancient palace area. Part of the new library actually sits underwater.

Others had been stabbed by paid killers. She also learned that there was no law stating who would become the next king or queen. Auletes, like the Ptolemies before him, would simply choose the next ruler from among his children and relatives.

In this world, Cleopatra learned she must always be on guard. She must watch her brothers and sisters carefully. They were just as ambitious as she was. If she lost the contest for power, she would also lose her life. If she won, she would have to get rid of the others. In this life-or-death struggle, she couldn't trust anyone. She was always being watched. Servants loyal to her brothers and sisters followed her around. They knew about her every movement, as she knew about theirs.

Cleopatra slowly became aware that Alexandrians hated her family. They thought the Ptolemies were greedy and corrupt. She saw crowds of angry people fighting with soldiers in the streets.

In this scary world, one fear outweighed all others. The Ptolemies feared that a foreign power

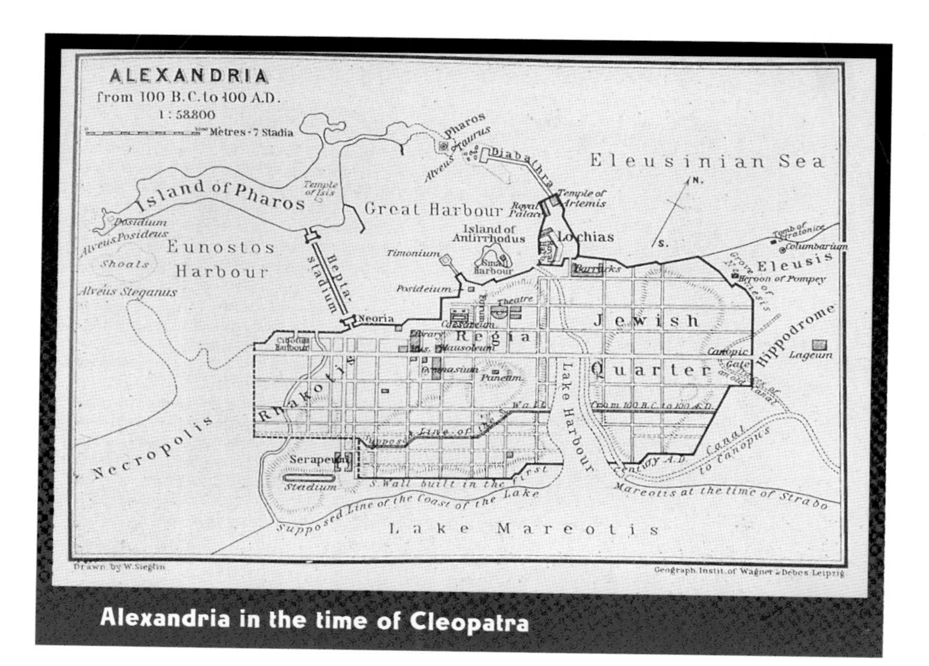

Alexandria in the time of Cleopatra

would take over their country. Auletes and his family knew that the Romans wanted to rule Egypt. Roman soldiers had already conquered ancient Greece and Macedonia. They controlled parts of North Africa and Asia Minor.

But the leaders of the Roman Republic waited before sending their armies into Egypt. Roman leaders didn't want any single Roman to hold too much power. They knew that the Roman who conquered Egypt would become very powerful. They worried that this powerful Roman might see himself as a king. He might turn his soldiers against the Roman Republic.

A Gang of Three

Meanwhile, the Roman Republic had changed. Military commanders had become more powerful. They kept hold of land they conquered. Their armies were personally loyal to them. These commanders enriched themselves with foreign wealth. At times, these generals grew strong enough to seize control of the entire Roman state.

In 65 B.C., the three most powerful generals were Julius Caesar, Pompey, and Crassus. In 60 B.C., they set up a triumvirate (a group of three rulers). Each was called a triumvir. These three shared the job of running the Roman state. The Triumvirate's actions brought the Roman Republic closer to becoming an empire—a territory under the control of a single leader.

The triumvirs needed the support of the Roman people to keep their power. To win that support, Caesar, Pompey, and Crassus each put on huge celebrations. Each wanted to show off his wealth. They held games and feasts for the public. At the same time, they each built up their armies to conquer more foreign land. Each worked hard to raise money. They had to support their armies, their public events, and their rich households.

In Egypt, Auletes saw that sooner or later Rome would bring its armies to Alexandria. They would seize the palace and its treasury. They would end the Ptolemaic dynasty. They would bring foreign rule and foreign taxes to the Egyptians. Auletes' greatest fear would be real.

Auletes decided to make a deal with the Romans. His goal was to keep his country independent. In 59 B.C., he offered the Triumvirate a huge bribe. (The money he offered equaled many millions of dollars in modern money.) The triumvirs gladly accepted the money. In exchange, they had the Roman Senate make an official statement. It said that Auletes was the "friend and ally of the Roman people." Because of Auletes' bribe, Egypt could stay free of Rome, at least for the time being.

But Auletes didn't have the money to pay this bribe. He had to borrow from a Roman moneylender named Rabirius. To pay the money back, he would have to heavily tax his people. While Auletes kept his throne, the economy of Egypt suffered. Many people starved for the sake of his corrupt dynasty.

When in Rome . . .

Auletes soon found that his bribe hadn't won him respect from the Romans. In 57 B.C., a Roman general named Cato seized the Egyptian-owned island of Cyprus. Auletes' brother ruled Cyprus. But the king of Egypt did nothing to save him. Rather than become a prisoner of the Romans, Auletes' brother committed suicide.

The people of Alexandria rebelled against Auletes for not helping his brother. Riots swept through the capital. The fighting reached the palace. Afraid for his life, Auletes fled in a ship bound for Rome. The Romans had declared him a "friend and ally." He believed he would be safe there. He believed the Romans might help him regain control of Egypt.

Auletes' daughter Berenice IV took this chance to proclaim herself Egypt's new ruler. Disgusted with Auletes, many Egyptian soldiers and diplomats allied with her. In Rome, Auletes promised an even larger bribe. The money would go to Pompey, Julius Caesar, and Governor Gabinius of Syria. In return, Gabinius agreed to attack Berenice IV. He would help bring Auletes back to power. Auletes left Rome, awaiting his daughter's defeat.

An engraving of Berenice IV, Cleopatra's older sister

Marching on Egypt

Gabinius declared war on Berenice IV. He led his large Roman army southward to Egypt. Rabirius, the moneylender, was with the army. He was anxious to get his share of Egypt's treasury. At the head of Gabinius's force was a twenty-five-year-old officer named Mark Antony.

Gabinius and Antony conquered the city of Pelusium on the eastern Egyptian border. Then they headed for Alexandria. There, they defeated the Egyptians fighting under the husband of Berenice IV.

The skilled Roman army scared the soldiers fighting for Berenice. They left her, and Gabinius took her prisoner. As soon as Auletes heard of his daughter's capture, he ordered her to be killed. Gabinius then pardoned the soldiers who had fought against Auletes. He ordered Roman soldiers to stay in Alexandria to protect the pharaoh. These soldiers came to be called Gabinians. They would make sure that Egypt repaid the bribes Auletes had promised to his Roman allies. Roman cargo ships were soon docking at Alexandria. They loaded cargoes of grain and chests of money for the trip back to Rome.

Just a few years later, in 51 B.C., Auletes died. In the meantime, he had given much thought to his successor. He knew Cleopatra VII had the skill to rule in his place. She was smart enough to keep the Romans at bay. But in ancient Egypt, a queen could not rule alone. She had to have a king. So Auletes decided that eighteen-year-old Cleopatra VII would rule the country with her half brother, ten-year-old Ptolemy XIII.

CHAPTER 3

Brother and Sister

As smart as she was, Cleopatra still had to share power with her little brother. Ptolemy was too young to match wits with Cleopatra. But he had three loyal, scheming advisers–Pothinus, Achillas, and Theodotus. These men worked to get Cleopatra off the throne. They even hoped to kill her. Their goal was to make Ptolemy the sole ruler of Egypt.

Pothinus ruled the servants and guards of the royal palace. Achillas commanded the Egyptian army. It was still one of the most powerful in the world. Theodotus was Ptolemy's tutor. He taught the young king how to deal with the Romans and with his older sister.

Cleopatra decided she must make herself known to the Egyptians. She wanted to show them that she would carry on their traditions. In March of 51 B.C., just after becoming queen, she traveled up the Nile to the city of Thebes. There she took part in a ceremony for the god Amon-Re.

This trip did not boost Cleopatra's popularity with the Egyptians. She and her half brother had come to power during a crisis. The yearly spring floods of the Nile had been poor. The harvests were small. People were starving. They grew restless and rebellious. Pothinus spread propaganda against Cleopatra. This propaganda made the people dislike her.

By 48 B.C., Cleopatra was beginning to fear Ptolemy's advisers. She fled Alexandria for Syria. She built up a small army there. And she waited for a chance to return.

Caesar and Pompey

Meanwhile, Crassus died. Rome's Triumvirate ended. Pompey and Caesar turned against each other. They began fighting a civil war. In 48 B.C., Caesar defeated Pompey. This victory made Caesar the most powerful leader in Rome. Caesar was fifty-four.

Julius Caesar was one of the greatest military leaders of all time. He was also a noted politician, writer, and public speaker.

He was ambitious, ruthless, and brilliant. He was admired for his courage in battle. His soldiers loved him for his generosity.

The beaten Pompey gathered an army. He sailed with it across the Mediterranean Sea to Egypt. He was looking for help from young Ptolemy XIII. Pompey planned to recruit the Gabinian Roman soldiers who were still living in Egypt. But Achillas, Pothinus, and Theodotus had different plans. They saw Caesar as the winner in the civil war. Pompey was the loser. They plotted to murder Pompey when he arrived in Egypt. They believed Caesar would be grateful. They believed he'd help them get rid of Cleopatra.

IT'S A FACT!

Pompey's wife was on board one of his ships that sailed to Alexandria. She sensed something wasn't right. She begged Pompey not to get in Ptolemy's boat. He ignored her. She watched in horror as her husband was stabbed in the back.

Pompey and his fleet arrived at the Egyptian coast. Ptolemy's military commander and a few soldiers sailed out to Pompey's ship. Pompey climbed in their boat. As the boat was rowed away, a Roman soldier loyal to Ptolemy stabbed Pompey in the back. His body was rowed ashore, where Pompey's head was cut off. Theodotus kept the head as a present for Julius Caesar.

FIGHTING FOR ALEXANDRIA

During this same time, Caesar had been chasing Pompey to Egypt. He was worried that Pompey would build a fresh army. Caesar planned to capture Alexandria and defeat Pompey once and for all. Caesar also intended to personally collect Auletes' debts.

After a four-day voyage, Caesar landed in Egypt. He had ten ships and four thousand soldiers. He easily captured Alexandria. When Caesar arrived at the palace, Theodotus greeted him with the head of Pompey. But instead of being grateful to Theodotus for this cold-blooded murder, Caesar scorned him. Caesar had been Pompey's enemy, but he was still a soldier. The miserable death that Pompey had suffered–stabbed in the back instead of honorably defeated in battle–angered Caesar.

Pothinus, Achillas, and Theodotus waited anxiously for Caesar to leave Egypt. But instead of returning to Rome, he decided to stay in the palace. He collected the money that Egypt still owed Rome. He convinced Pompey's soldiers to come over to his side. Caesar forgave them for fighting against him in the civil war.

Caesar decided to end the feud between Ptolemy and Cleopatra. He wanted them to rule Egypt together, as their father had wished. By bringing about peace, Caesar believed he would make himself and Rome even stronger. He and Rome would be able to collect taxes from the Egyptians. Best of all, he would bring peace without having to fight a single battle.

But Ptolemy's three advisers weren't interested. If Rome controlled Alexandria, their own power would decline. So they plotted to get Caesar and his army out of Alexandria. Achillas made life hard for the Romans. He ordered moldy grain to be delivered to the Roman soldiers. He stirred up anti-Roman feelings among the Alexandrians. Street battles broke out between the citizens and Roman soldiers. Many people were killed. Meanwhile, Achillas's army kept watch for Cleopatra's return to Egypt.

Sneaking In

Caesar ordered Ptolemy and Cleopatra to come to the palace. But Cleopatra would have to pass Achillas's army to reach the palace grounds. She knew that if Achillas's men caught her, they would kill her.

Cleopatra came up with a plan to sneak into Alexandria. She set off in a small boat with a merchant named Apollodorus. After reaching Alexandria, Cleopatra and Apollodorus sailed into the harbor near the palace. Apollodorus then rolled up Cleopatra in a carpet.

Roman soldiers and Egyptian guards closely watched the doors of the palace. Apollodorus,

According to legend, Julius Caesar was pleasantly surprised when the twenty-one-year-old Cleopatra rolled out of a carpet to greet him.

dressed as a servant, passed the guards with a heavy bundle thrown over his shoulder. In this way, he brought Cleopatra safely into Caesar's chamber. There, while Caesar and his many guards watched, he unrolled the carpet. The queen of Egypt tumbled out at Caesar's feet.

Cleopatra was only twenty-one years old. But her cleverness fascinated Caesar. He found her intelligence more interesting than her beauty. He was married to a Roman named Calpurnia. But within a few days, Caesar and Cleopatra became lovers.

Who Knows?

In many ways, Cleopatra is still a mystery. Historians know about her actions only through Greek and Roman writings. Nobody set down Cleopatra's own words. Even her appearance is a mystery. Small, faded coins made in Cleopatra's time show only one side of her face. She had a strong chin, heavy brows, and a large hooked nose. A few busts of Egyptian women from her time may show her. But no one's really sure. Several ancient historians wrote descriptions of Cleopatra. Most of them lived after her time, however. They could write down only what others had told them about her.

The Roman writer Plutarch heard descriptions of Cleopatra. Members of his family had known her. In one of his books, Plutarch reported that "her actual beauty . . . was not in itself so remarkable . . . but . . . the attraction of her person, joining with the charm of her conversation . . . was something bewitching. It was a pleasure merely to hear the sound of her voice."

Source of quote: Plutarch, *Lives of the Noble Grecians and Romans* (New York: Random House, n.d.), 1,119.

A Turn for the Worse

Caesar ordered Ptolemy to get along with his sister. He asked the two to rule Egypt jointly. Cleopatra agreed, because she knew Caesar supported her. On the advice of Pothinus, Ptolemy also agreed. But the boy was only trying to buy time. He knew Caesar was loyal to Cleopatra. Ptolemy would wait for Caesar to leave Egypt. Then he'd try once again to grab power for himself.

Cleopatra watched and waited. She knew that she would never be able to rule peacefully with her half brother. His advisers were still determined to get rid of her. Pothinus had turned most of Egypt against her. Achillas controlled the Egyptian army. Cleopatra could do nothing until Caesar defeated Ptolemy and his advisers.

Achillas knew Caesar backed Cleopatra. Caesar wouldn't leave unless he was driven back to Rome. Later that year, Achillas sent an army of twenty thousand men to march on Alexandria. The army occupied the city and surrounded the palace. Caesar seemed to be caught in a trap. So the Alexandrians began rioting against the Roman

IT'S A FACT!

In general, Ptolemaic queens were second in power to the king. But Cleopatra often ignored Ptolemy XIII and his advisers. She believed her skills as a ruler were better than theirs. She made political decisions on her own. She kept Ptolemy from public events. Cleopatra even had coins made that only showed her face on them.

soldiers. Inside the palace, the Roman guards closely watched Cleopatra, Ptolemy, and Pothinus. They also watched Arsinoë IV, Cleopatra's younger half sister. As long as Caesar's army held out, none of the royal family would be harmed. But Caesar would allow none of them to leave.

The standoff continued. Convinced that Caesar would lose, Arsinoë IV slipped out of the palace. She joined Achillas in the camps. She named herself the new queen of Egypt. She would rule along with Ptolemy XIII. Pothinus and Ptolemy made plans to join Arsinoë IV. But word of the plan soon leaked to Caesar. Suspecting that Pothinus was planning to kill him, Caesar ordered his arrest. The adviser was put to death for treason.

Queen of Egypt

Caesar's guards controlled the inside of the palace. His troops fought in the streets against Achillas's men. Caesar himself led the fight, both on land and in the harbor. While battles raged between Roman and Egyptian battleships, Cleopatra watched from the palace.

In the meantime, Arsinoë IV quarreled with Achillas. Her adviser, Ganymedes, ordered her guards to kill Achillas. After Achillas was murdered, Ganymedes took control of the army. He continued the attack on the palace and on the Roman ships.

Caesar searched for a way to beat the Egyptian army. Cleopatra may have given him an idea. She suggested he allow Ptolemy to leave the palace. Cleopatra and Caesar knew that Ptolemy would join Arsinoë IV and Ganymedes. Cleopatra and Caesar bet that the three of them would quarrel. The Egyptian army would become a target for a surprise attack.

In the meantime, more Roman troops began arriving in Egypt from Syria. These troops attacked the Egyptians from the east. On March 27 of 47 B.C., Caesar fought back. He and his army battled the Egyptians along the shores of Lake Mareotis. The Egyptians outnumbered the Roman soldiers. Yet, the Romans fought with discipline. They easily defeated the Egyptian troops. Many Egyptians ran for their lives. The Roman troops killed enemy survivors. Meanwhile, fourteen-year-old Ptolemy XIII drowned in the Nile River while fleeing.

Soon after the battle, Caesar's troops took Arsinoë IV prisoner. Caesar had become the master of Egypt. But ruling Egypt didn't interest him. He trusted Cleopatra to rule Egypt as his ally. At twenty-two years old, she was smart and wise.

It's a Fact!

Cleopatra was highly educated. As she grew older, she became a scholar. She wrote books on medicine, math, and even makeup. Some sources suggest she led talks with scientists.

But, according to custom, a queen needed a king. At Caesar's direction, Cleopatra married her youngest half brother, Ptolemy XIV. Cleopatra made sure that this Ptolemy had no scheming advisers. Only twelve years old, he was too young to fight his half sister.

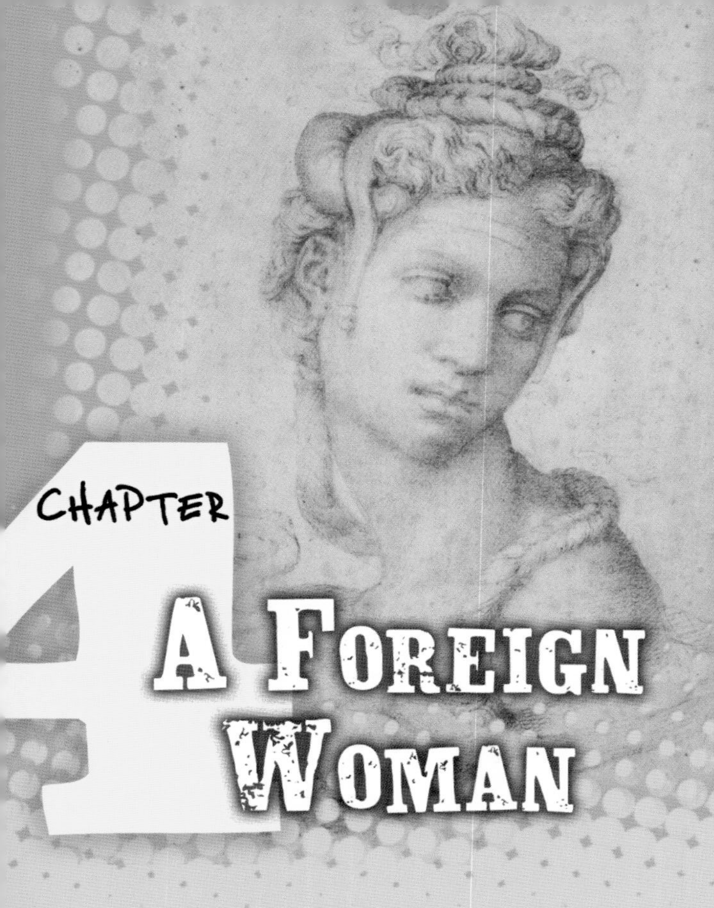

CHAPTER 4 A FOREIGN WOMAN

INSTEAD OF RETURNING immediately to Rome, Caesar stayed in Egypt. He decided to enjoy a few months of relaxation. Cleopatra was determined to amuse Caesar. She wanted to strengthen her ties to him. She ordered her servants to prepare her royal barge for a trip. It would take the lovers up the Nile River. The boat was huge. According to some ancient historians, the ship was 300 feet (91 m) long.

Cleopatra *(above)* knew that Caesar was the key to keeping her power in Egypt. This drawing is from the 1500s.

Marble and gold decorated it. The boat had lavish dining halls and bedrooms.

Some of Caesar's army sailed alongside the barge. The lovers stopped at cities and temples along the Nile. Crowds gathered at the riverbank to watch them. Cleopatra proudly stood at Caesar's side. She wanted to show her subjects that she was the queen of Egypt. She also wanted to show Egyptians that she was the ally of Rome's strongest leader. It didn't hurt that she was also pregnant with Caesar's child. (The child, a boy named Caesarion, would be born a few months later.)

Caesar and Cleopatra may have been in love. But they were also practical and clever. Each found the other a useful partner. They had a goal in common. They both wanted more power. They

Grand Plans

Cleopatra and Caesar may have been planning to start an entirely new dynasty. Caesarion was born on June 23, 47 B.C. The new family of rulers would combine the Ptolemies with Caesar's Roman family. Joined together, Egypt and Rome would form an empire even larger than the one Alexander the Great had conquered. Caesarion would be the first king of this new empire. Its capital city would be Alexandria.

needed each other to reach their goals. Cleopatra needed Rome's protection. And Caesar needed to have influence over Egypt and its wealth.

The Triumphs of Caesar

After the romantic Nile trip, Caesar could no longer put off returning to Rome. Following a sad farewell, Caesar sailed home. He left behind more than fifty thousand troops to keep order in Alexandria. He told the troops to support Cleopatra against rivals within and outside of Egypt.

In September of 46 B.C., Caesar celebrated his latest military victories in Rome. He held military parades, called triumphs. His soldiers marched through the center of the city. The Romans cheered. Prisoners of war walked in chains behind the army.

It's a Fact!

The fanciest of Caesar's triumphs celebrated his victory against the Egyptians. Shuffling along in chains at the head of the prisoners was Cleopatra's half sister Arsinoë IV. By tradition, prisoners were killed after the ceremonies. But the humiliation of the young Egyptian princess angered some Roman citizens. For this reason, Caesar decided to let Arsinoë live.

After one triumph, Caesar invited Cleopatra to visit Rome as an independent ruler and ally. Cleopatra sailed to Rome with Caesarion. She also took young Ptolemy XIV with her. Her idea was to keep him out of trouble. She moved into Caesar's palace.

To honor Cleopatra, Caesar built a temple dedicated to the Roman goddess Venus. She was the goddess of love. Next to Venus, he put up a

Cleopatra as Isis

Queen Cleopatra continued the Egyptian tradition of ruler-god. She identified herself with the goddess Isis. Egyptians believed Isis made the Nile rise each year. They believed she brought good harvests. Cleopatra ordered Egyptian sculptors to carve her as Isis. Egyptian coins showed her as the goddess. When Cleopatra appeared in public, she wore a royal crown that included carved snakes and the moon. The snakes stood for Amon-Re. The moon was the symbol of Isis.

This statuette of Isis and her son, Horus, was made long before Cleopatra's time.

statue of Cleopatra. The statue showed the queen as the Egyptian goddess Isis. Egyptians had long thought of their rulers as gods. But the Romans did not. Caesar's statue angered the Romans. They suspected Cleopatra of using Caesar to reach her own goals.

The Royal Family

To the people of Rome, Cleopatra was no goddess. She was a foreigner. She was an Egyptian descended from Macedonian Greeks. Worse, she was a woman who held total royal power. This level of authority was unknown in Rome's history.

Caesar was a married man. His legal wife was Calpurnia. Under Roman law, he couldn't have more than one wife. Yet the Romans didn't object to Caesar having an affair with Cleopatra. After all, he had defeated the Egyptian army. They believed he could do whatever he liked with the losers. But the Romans were concerned about him inviting a foreign queen to live in Rome. They really had trouble with his raising a statue to her in the center of the city.

Caesar's actions angered Rome's patricians (upper-class members of Roman society). Caesar,

An Egyptian stone carving of Cleopatra (*left*) with her son (*right*). Realizing that Caesar was the father, the Alexandrians called the child Caesarion, or Little Caesar.

Cleopatra, and Caesarion were acting like a royal family. The patricians felt that Caesar was behaving as if he might create a kingdom or empire. (In this type of government, rulers govern alone and choose their own successors.) The patricians ruled the Roman Republic in the Senate. Under this system, no king or emperor ruled. The Senate made all laws. Sometimes, the senators named consuls, or chief lawmakers.

But Roman soldiers and common citizens still felt a strong loyalty to Caesar. He had fought and won many battles. He had captured huge amounts of land in Europe and Asia. Shortly after the triumphs of Caesar, the Senate named him the only consul of Rome for five years.

Caesar used his power to expel senators who opposed him. He replaced them with his friends. At Cleopatra's urging, he had the Senate officially declare Cleopatra and Ptolemy to be the "Friends and Allies of Rome." Slowly but surely, Caesar was turning the Roman Republic into an empire. Obviously, he would be this new empire's ruler. Most Romans hated the idea of the republic being ruled by one person.

Paying No Attention

Caesar still felt restless. He was a soldier. And soldiers fought battles. He looked for new enemies to conquer. In the spring of 45 B.C., he defeated Pompey's sons at Munda, in modern Spain. In early 44 B.C., he prepared for a series of battles against Parthia. (This powerful ancient empire covered what has since become northeastern Iran.) No one had been able to take control of Parthia. And several Roman generals had tried. Anyone who could defeat the Parthians would be seen as a military leader as fine as Alexander the Great.

Caesar planned to leave Rome around the Ides (fifteenth) of March. Cleopatra didn't want to stay in the city without him. She had many enemies among the patricians and among Caesar's rivals. Cleopatra made plans to return to Egypt.

At the same time, several leading Romans talked secretly about ending Caesar's life. Two men–named Brutus and Cassius–came up with a plot to kill Caesar. The plotters believed that Caesar would soon name himself emperor.

The death of Julius Caesar painted in 1793 by Italian artist Vincenzo Camuccini

Rumors of the plot were everywhere. Friends warned Caesar, but he ignored them. He had faced many plots against his life and had not been killed. In Rome, the people seemed to adore him. They supported his every action. He felt safe.

On the Ides of March, 44 B.C., Brutus, Cassius, and more than twenty senators gathered in the Senate hall. Caesar entered the hall. The entire group of Senate plotters crowded around him. Each held a knife under his cloak. At a signal, they ran forward, stabbing Caesar in a frenzy. He desperately fought them off. But he had too many stab wounds to live. Within minutes, Caesar was dead.

IT'S A FACT!

At first, Caesar decided not to go to the Senate on the Ides of March. His wife, Calpurnia, had had bad dreams about the idea. But he changed his mind after talking with Brutus. Brutus told him that he would be made king of all Roman provinces that day. "Beware the Ides of March!" is a famous saying. It means that someone senses danger.

CHAPTER 5

CLEOPATRA AND ANTONY

AMONG THE PEOPLE, Caesar was a hero. With his death, he had become a martyr (a person who has sacrificed his own life). Mobs rioted in Rome. They hunted down and murdered many of Caesar's killers. Brutus and Cassius fled the city. They eventually went to Greece to build up their armies.

A messenger brought Cleopatra the news of Caesar's death. She and Caesarion were alone in a foreign city. Cleopatra believed they were in great danger. She rushed to Ostia, the port of Rome. From there, she and her son sailed home.

Shortly after she arrived in Alexandria, Ptolemy XIV was murdered. Cleopatra may

Mark Antony addresses the Romans at the body of Julius Caesar.

have ordered the deed. She then named Caesarion as Ptolemy XV Caesar, her new co-ruler. She believed that placing her half-Roman son at her side would strengthen her ties to the future leader of Rome, whoever he might be.

In the meantime, Caesar's funeral had taken place in Rome. Mark Antony, Caesar's friend, had given a moving speech. The crowds admired Antony's speech. It talked about the sadness that many of them were feeling.

IT'S A FACT!

Cleopatra named her son, Caesarion, as co-ruler. By tradition, the two became legally married so that he could be king. He was just three years old at the time.

Octavius, Julius Caesar's great nephew, was running the funeral. This young man was preparing himself to succeed his great-uncle as Rome's next leader. In his will, Caesar had named the nineteen-year-old Octavius his heir. In 43 B.C., Antony allied with Octavius and Marcus Lepidus. Antony, Octavius, and Lepidus agreed to form the Second Triumvirate.

It's a Fact!

Caesar had not mentioned Cleopatra or Caesarion in his will. By Roman law, foreigners could not inherit Roman property.

Choosing Sides

Each of the triumvirs then drew up a list of their enemies. They accused several thousand people of plotting against Caesar. On the triumvirs' orders, the lands and money of the accused plotters were taken away. Hundreds of accused plotters were murdered. With the money, Antony raised an army to fight Brutus and Cassius. Brutus was in Greece, raising an army. Cassius was with land troops in Syria. Both sides in this new civil war needed ships and soldiers. Both sides wanted help from Cleopatra.

Cleopatra knew that she must choose carefully. If she helped the winner of this war, she and Caesarion would remain in control of Egypt. If she sent help to the side that lost, the winners would take over Egypt.

Cleopatra decided to side with the Triumvirate against Brutus and Cassius. The triumvirs had won her friendship by recognizing Caesarion as her co-ruler. Cleopatra prepared the Egyptian army to sail to Greece to fight Brutus. She also sent Caesar's Roman soldiers in Egypt to march against Cassius in Syria. Cleopatra sent a message to Cassius. She said that famine was raging through Egypt. It was impossible for her to send aid.

Cassius was angry and determined to punish the queen. He ordered his soldiers to march south and invade Egypt. But soon, Brutus sent Cassius an urgent message. The triumvirs were sailing toward Greece. Brutus and Cassius then marched to Macedonia. They prepared to face Antony, Octavius, and Lepidus in battle in Alexander the Great's homeland.

Cleopatra realized that a battle would soon take place. She prepared a fleet of Egyptian warships to set sail from Alexandria. She rode in the main ship. She ordered the fleet to sail toward Greece. But within a few days, the fleet ran into a heavy storm. Several Egyptian ships were lost. Cleopatra became ill. She ordered her ships to return to Alexandria.

Dividing Up Roman Lands

In October of 42 B.C., the triumvirs defeated Cassius and Brutus in Greece. Both men committed suicide. They'd rather die in their own way than be captured and killed. The victors celebrated by dividing Rome's territory among the three of them. Octavius would rule Rome and the western Mediterranean. Antony would rule the eastern Mediterranean–Greece, Asia Minor, and Syria. Lepidus would have the Roman provinces of North Africa.

To most Romans, Antony seemed to be the true heir of Julius Caesar. He had their loyalty. Antony's armies were large. He was mature and strong. He was an experienced military commander. Octavius, on the other hand, was young. He had spent most of his life studying. He had no experience of war or leadership.

Yet Caesar had trusted Octavius enough to name him as his heir. Caesar knew Octavius had no experience leading soldiers or citizens. But Caesar had believed the young man was clever enough to handle his enemies.

Cleopatra soon heard of the victory of the triumvirs. She remembered Antony. He had helped Gabinius beat Cleopatra's sister Berenice IV. But this time, Cleopatra was looking for the long-term winner. She thought Antony was the strongest man in Rome. Someday, the Triumvirate would end. Someday, she believed, Antony would become Rome's sole leader.

The New Leader

Mark Antony had enjoyed his youth. He had that certain something that drew people to him. He was friendly and outgoing. He paid for lavish parties. He hung out with actors and musicians. His behavior shocked the patricians.

Antony liked physical goals more than intellectual ones. But, after a time, he settled down. He

It's a Fact!

Julius Caesar had been a gifted writer, as well as a skilled general. In contrast, Mark Antony was loud, with a rude sense of humor.

became one of the most popular leaders in the Roman armies. Writers described him as noble and manly in appearance. But he also showed good people skills. He'd eat with his soldiers, rather than with the other generals. Like his soldiers, he could be rowdy. He was kind to his friends.

In 41 B.C., Antony traveled to Greece and Asia Minor. Crowds hailed him as the new emperor. They worshipped him as a ruler-god. Antony gathered musicians and entertainers to put on grand events in the cities he ruled. To pay for his celebrations–as well as to pay his army–he heavily taxed Rome's lands in the eastern Mediterranean.

Antony had not yet finished conquering new lands. He was preparing to take up Caesar's battle against Parthia. Parthia's defeat would take out the last major kingdom that was resisting Rome. Antony wanted to show everyone that he, rather than Octavius, was worthy to succeed Julius Caesar.

Antony reached the city of Tarsus, along the Cydnus River. He ordered Cleopatra to meet him there. He wanted her to explain a rumor that she had secretly helped Cassius in the civil war. Antony also wanted her to promise her support to his Parthian campaign.

Mark Antony sees Cleopatra on her royal barge in this painting from the late 1800s.

Cleopatra saw a chance to impress Antony with her wealth and glamour. She arrived aboard her huge barge. She then sent word that Antony should come to the riverside to meet her. After some hesitation, Antony agreed. He would come to the barge and look like he was Cleopatra's guest. Aboard the barge, Cleopatra treated him to a dazzling sight. She had dressed as Aphrodite, the Greek goddess of love and beauty. She hosted a lavish banquet for Antony and his soldiers. The next night, Antony returned the favor, holding a banquet for the queen.

Striking Bargains

Cleopatra understood men. She understood Roman men in particular. She saw that Mark Antony could be just as useful to her as Julius Caesar had been. Antony commanded the largest army in Rome. He also had the support of Rome's common people and its patricians. Even better, Antony controlled the eastern half of Rome's territories. Cleopatra wanted to build her empire there, with Antony. Next to him, Octavius looked like a young boy.

It's a Fact!

Cleopatra is often described as a seducer of men. But historical records say that she had love affairs with only Julius Caesar and Mark Antony.

Instantly fascinated by each other, Cleopatra and Mark Antony became lovers. Antony returned with Cleopatra to Alexandria. She and her lavish lifestyle charmed him. She, in turn, must have been attracted to his strength, courage, and good humor. They held wild parties in the palace. They ran around the streets of Alexandria disguised as servants. They roamed the city and played pranks on the people they met.

The lovers also struck a political deal. Antony needed Cleopatra's help in his campaign to attack Parthia. Cleopatra promised to supply soldiers and money. In return, Antony promised to order the murder of Arsinoë IV. She was hiding in Asia Minor. Soon Arsinoë IV–Cleopatra's only living sister or brother–was dead.

Antony spent the winter in Alexandria. Then he returned to Rome to settle conflicts with other members of the Triumvirate. In October 40 B.C., he made an agreement with Octavius. The two men would keep the division between eastern and western Rome just as it was. They would also allow Lepidus, the weakest triumvir, to continue governing the less wealthy North African territories. To seal the deal, Antony married Octavius's beautiful and kind sister, Octavia. (Patricians often set up a marriage to show goodwill or to complete an agreement.)

The news of Antony's marriage hurt Cleopatra. The twenty-nine-year-old queen turned to her own affairs in Egypt. Her alliance with Antony made sure that she could rule Egypt without Roman interference. She also held a claim on Antony's loyalty in the future. Earlier in the year, she had given birth to Antony's twins. She named them Alexander Helios and Cleopatra Selene. Cleopatra saw her children by Caesar and Antony as heirs to the Roman-Egyptian dynasty that she still hoped to start in Alexandria.

In Charge

For the next three and a half years, Cleopatra ably ruled her kingdom alone. The Egyptian economy revived after a period of drought. Peace gave traders a chance to carry on business without trouble. The Egyptian treasury recovered from the heavy payments Cleopatra's father had promised the Romans. Unlike her father, Cleopatra carefully

Just Like Captain Picard

In 2000, a scientist found what may be an actual sample of Cleopatra's handwriting. A business order had been written on a piece of paper. The paper had been stuffed inside an ancient Egyptian container. Beneath the order, in different handwriting, was the word *ginesthoi.* This word means "make it so." A pharaoh would use this word to confirm an order. The paper dates from 33 B.C., during Cleopatra's reign.

managed Egypt's finances. She worked hard to increase harvests.

Cleopatra took care to observe religious traditions. She identified herself in artwork as Isis. She supported religious temples through gifts of food and money. For the first time, a Ptolemaic ruler could speak and write Egyptian. The people admired Cleopatra for her diplomacy. They liked her plan to keep Egypt out of Rome's way.

No one opposed Cleopatra's rule. The uprisings common in her father's time had stopped. All her brothers and sisters had died in battle or by murder. The army remained loyal to the queen. She also had Antony's support, so no foreigner dared to attack her. Meanwhile, tutors and advisers prepared her children for the responsibilities that awaited them.

Uneasy Alliances

In 37 B.C., Antony and Octavius made another agreement. Octavius, Antony, and Lepidus would continue as triumvirs. Antony would send ships to help Octavius fight the ruler of Sicily, an island south of Rome. In return, Octavius agreed to send soldiers to join Antony's campaigns against Parthia.

Despite the treaty, many people in Rome saw that the Roman world was not big enough for Antony and Octavius. Each meeting between them started rumors of another civil war. Antony was growing uneasy about Octavius in Rome. Antony and his wife, Octavia, left for his lands in the eastern Mediterranean. On the way, Octavia grew ill. She was pregnant with Antony's child. She would not join him in any military campaigns. For Octavia's sake, Antony sent her back to Rome. Many Romans falsely assumed that she was sent home because Antony had rejected her. Octavius, Octavia's brother, took Antony's action as an insult.

Antony continued on to Syria. He had not seen Cleopatra in years. But he sent her a message asking her to join him. Cleopatra had waited for this moment. She left Egypt for Syria right away. There, the two may have gotten married. The ceremony would have shocked many Romans. Roman law prohibited marriage to more than one person. Antony and Cleopatra began appearing together on coins in Asia Minor and Egypt.

Both leaders were always politically minded. They had struck a bargain. Cleopatra agreed to build a fleet of ships for Antony. She also would

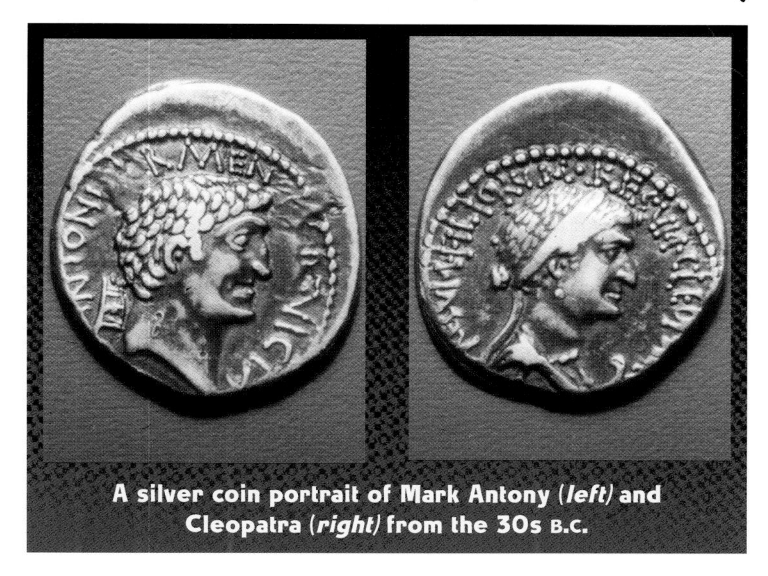

A silver coin portrait of Mark Antony *(left)* and Cleopatra *(right)* from the 30s B.C.

keep her promise to support Antony's campaign in Parthia with money and soldiers. In return, Antony agreed to turn over most of his eastern territories–including Asia Minor, the island of Cyprus, Phoenicia (modern Lebanon), and Jordan–to her.

With this grant of land, Antony made Cleopatra the queen of one of the largest Egyptian realms in history. Her rule included many rich cities in the Middle East. The forests of Asia Minor and Phoenicia would supply the wood for an Egyptian fleet of warships.

Antony's gifts helped his alliance with Cleopatra. But they caused a scandal in Rome. To the Romans, Antony had no right to give away what was not his. He had given Roman territories to a foreigner. Octavius and his friends did nothing to calm the outrage many Romans felt over these acts.

Antony's Campaign

After several years of planning, Antony was finally prepared to march into Parthia. He was sure that his army would succeed. In the spring of 36 B.C., the Romans began their invasion. Antony divided his forces in two–the main army and a baggage train. The baggage train contained Antony's siege equipment, such as catapults, battering rams, and towers. He would need this equipment to defeat the walled Parthian cities. The main army forged ahead. The Parthian army suddenly attacked the slower-moving baggage train. The soldiers destroyed the siege equipment and killed thousands of Roman soldiers. Many other Romans deserted.

Antony was forced to halt his land army before he ever entered Parthia. Without siege equipment, he could do nothing. Worse, winter was coming. His army was running out of food.

In October 36 B.C., Antony turned back toward Syria. During the retreat, hit-and-run attacks, disease, and hunger killed thousands of Roman soldiers. By the time Antony's once-proud army reached Syria, nearly half of the troops were dead.

Antony had wanted to beat Parthia to win glory for his army. But the campaign had ended in total failure. No one saw him as the equal of Alexander the Great or Julius Caesar.

CHAPTER 6
RULING TOGETHER IN EGYPT

MESSENGERS BROUGHT NEWS to Egypt of the failed campaign. Antony soon sent for Cleopatra. She had just given birth to his son Ptolemy Philadelphus. In January of 35 B.C., Cleopatra arrived in Syria. She brought winter clothing and money for Antony's soldiers. Later that year, Antony and Cleopatra returned to Alexandria. Antony got ready for another military campaign. After the Parthian loss, he needed to reestablish himself as a successful military leader.

Choosing Egypt

Meanwhile, Antony's wife, Octavia, also heard about the failed campaign. So had her brother, Octavius. His power in Rome was increasing. He urged his sister to go to Egypt. She set out from Rome, taking ships and troops that he supplied. Octavia wanted to bring Antony back to Rome. She also wanted him to make up with her brother. Before she could reach Egypt, Antony sent her a message. She was to send the ships to Egypt. But he ordered Octavia to turn back to Rome. Antony had decided to remain with Cleopatra.

It's a Fact!

Octavius never sent the twenty thousand soldiers he had promised Antony. His decision may have been a reaction to Antony sending Octavia back to Rome. In any case, Cleopatra's help became even more valuable to Antony.

Antony may have made this decision out of

fear of Octavius's growing power. Octavius had recently taken over the island of Sicily. He had had a disagreement with Lepidus, the weakest triumvir. Octavius expelled Lepidus and ended the Triumvirate. If Octavius was strong enough to get rid of Lepidus, what would he do if Antony returned?

Antony knew that he could trust Cleopatra. She had proven her loyalty to him. She also ruled a wealthy country. Egypt could give him limitless money, soldiers, and glory. Antony could continue to compete with Octavius for power. Or he could live as a pharaoh in Cleopatra's country.

Antony and Cleopatra began another round of parties. She wanted Antony to stay in Alexandria. So she poured attention and glory upon him. Together, they posed as gods in religious ceremonies. They led parades through the streets of Alexandria. Cleopatra

It's a Fact!

Cleopatra and Antony enjoyed lavish parties. At one point, the queen ordered eight wild boars to be prepared throughout one evening. Each would feed about a dozen people. She wanted one perfectly cooked boar to be available the moment Antony wanted to eat.

Antony and Cleopatra enjoy a feast in this painting from the early 1700s.

turned her home into a pleasure palace. Music, dancing, and feasting took place nonstop.

The Donations of Alexandria

Antony was still determined to achieve a military victory. He had to wipe out the memory of his defeat in Parthia. He chose to march on Armenia, a small kingdom north of Parthia. Antony defeated and captured Artavasdes, the Armenian king in 34 B.C. Antony brought Artavasdes back to Alexandria. He displayed the king as a prisoner in a grand celebration. Antony held public banquets and gave away money as part of the festivities. He and Cleopatra paraded through the streets dressed as gods.

A few days later, Antony and Cleopatra held another public ceremony. They sat on golden thrones. In front of a crowd, they affirmed that Cleopatra was queen of Egypt, Cyprus, and the southern part of Syria. They also named their children heirs to the Roman provinces of the eastern Mediterranean.

Their son Ptolemy Philadelphus would rule northern Syria and several small kingdoms in Asia Minor. Alexander Helios would control Armenia, Media (northwestern Iran), and Parthia (which Antony had yet to conquer). Cleopatra Selene got Cyrene (part of modern-day Libya) and the island of Crete. Antony also declared that Caesarion, not Octavius, was Caesar's heir. Antony and Cleopatra obviously meant to take Rome from Octavius. Someday, Caesarion would rule Rome and the western Mediterranean.

The public ceremony came to be known as the Donations of Alexandria. The declarations were

Antony's way of paying back Cleopatra for her ongoing support. The ceremony was Cleopatra's way of claiming Antony as her co-ruler. Cleopatra had enlarged the Ptolemaic empire. It was much larger than any territory the previous pharaohs had ever ruled. But the Donations of Alexandria would be true only if she and Antony could keep holding these lands.

Propaganda

To Cleopatra, the Donations of Alexandria were the beginning of a new dynasty in Alexandria. For the Romans, it symbolized something else entirely. If Antony and Cleopatra succeeded, Rome's hold over the Mediterranean world would end.

Octavius knew how to turn these events to his advantage. He started a propaganda campaign against Antony and Cleopatra. Octavius announced that the Donations of Alexandria had given away Roman territories. This act made Antony a traitor to Rome. Octavius said Antony ruled the eastern provinces only for himself, not for the Roman people. Love for Cleopatra had blinded Antony. Cleopatra wanted to turn Alexandria into the new Rome.

Octavius *(left)* convinced the Romans that Antony was under Cleopatra's evil influence. Octavius said the lovers should both be defeated by force.

Octavius then told the Romans what he claimed was in Mark Antony's will. He said Antony wished to be buried in Egypt. This wish was a serious insult to Rome. Antony, Octavius said, had declared his children by Cleopatra to be his heirs, rather than those he had had by Octavia. Whether or not Antony's will said these things, Octavius made his point. Some Romans were still loyal to Antony. But many came to see him as an enemy of Rome.

Antony had gripes against Octavius too. Octavius had promised to send thousands of troops to help Antony in his Parthian campaign. He sent only a few thousand. Octavius had dismissed Lepidus without talking with Antony first. Octavius had not returned Antony's ships, which Octavius had borrowed to take Sicily. To answer Octavius's insults, Antony divorced Octavia.

This battle of personalities broke the ties between Antony and Octavius. As the people of

Noble Octavia

Octavia was the sister of Octavius. At a young age, she married a former consul of Rome. After his death, the Senate ordered her to marry Mark Antony. She was Antony's fourth wife. The marriage was to form an alliance between Antony and Octavius. Both men were triumvirs. During her marriage, Octavia raised Antony's children from his previous marriages. She also gave birth to two daughters by him. Unlike other noble women of the time, Octavia didn't scheme against her husband or family. She was loyal and kind.

Rome and Egypt could plainly see, Antony had made his choice. He would stay with Cleopatra in Egypt. And, as a result, he was no longer welcome in Rome. Sooner or later, the two men would fight each other. They began gathering their forces. Both knew a battle was coming.

Preparing for War

Antony prepared for the showdown. In 33 B.C., Antony and Cleopatra settled in Ephesus, a city in Asia Minor. They put together a fleet of more than five hundred ships. Skilled Greek crews manned the ships. Cleopatra ordered servants to store her huge treasury of gold and jewelry aboard her royal flagship. Cleopatra's treasury would help Antony pay and supply his troops.

Antony gathered an army of more than one hundred thousand troops. Early in the next year, nearly three hundred of the nine hundred Roman senators left Rome to show their support for Antony. Antony had a large army. He had much greater skill as a general. He seemed to be the likely winner in the coming battle. These senators wanted to be on his side. Antony and Cleopatra felt sure they'd win against Octavius. They traveled

Cleopatra on a gold coin of the 30s B.C. Her gold helped pay for Antony's troops.

slowly across Greece and toward Rome. They stopped at the island of Samos, where they partied and held banquets.

From Samos, Antony and Cleopatra sailed across the Aegean Sea to Athens, Greece. Antony knew that he could defeat Octavius in a land battle. After all, his army was much larger than Octavius's. Antony decided not to continue on to Rome. He knew that, for many Romans, Cleopatra posed a threat. If they went together to Rome, it would look like an attack on the city. If she and Antony defeated Octavius, she would become queen of Rome as well as of Egypt. Many of the Roman senators and generals at Antony's side told him that Cleopatra was making him unpopular. It might be best, some hinted, if Cleopatra returned to Egypt. Antony could face his rival alone. Others suggested something much different. Antony should have the queen murdered and claim Egypt for himself.

Cleopatra refused to leave Antony's side. If she returned to Egypt, she announced, her navy and her treasury would go with her. Antony chose to keep

Mark Antony

Cleopatra with him. He would wait for Octavius in Greece. A final battle on this neutral ground would decide the future of Rome and Egypt.

In Rome, Octavius prepared for the battle. In 32 B.C., he declared war–not on Antony but on Cleopatra. Octavius believed this action would bring more Romans to his side. Octavius arranged for the Senate to dismiss Antony as a triumvir.

Octavius led a parade to the temple of Bellona, the Roman goddess of war. Following tradition, he threw a bloodstained spear. He pointed it eastward, in the direction of the enemy. The Romans cheered. Octavius's army then marched southward to Brundisium and Tarentum. These ports were across the Ionian Sea from Greece. The troops set up camp for the winter. Octavius's commanders got their crews ready for the upcoming battles.

CHAPTER 7

THE BATTLE OF ACTIUM

MEANWHILE, CLEOPATRA and Antony moved their forces to western Greece, across the Ionian Sea from Italy. They split up their navy. They sent the fleets to patrol the Ionian seacoast. Most of their ships were in the well-protected Gulf of Ambracia. A smaller fleet stayed near the island of Corfu. Another fleet was at the southwestern tip of Greece. Antony placed troops along the southern shore of the gulf, which was marshy. The area was full of mosquitoes, which carry malaria. On land, behind the gulf, was a narrow point called Actium.

Octavius named Marcus Agrippa, his top commander, to lead the campaign against Antony and Cleopatra. Agrippa learned they had divided their forces. He decided to attack them piece by piece. In March of 31 B.C., he defeated Antony and Cleopatra's fleet at the southwestern tip of Greece. Using this area as his headquarters, Agrippa cut off Antony and Cleopatra from any supplies from Egypt. To keep from starving, Antony's soldiers took what they could from the barren mountain valleys near the gulf.

A portrait of Marcus Agrippa, Octavius's top commander

It's a Fact!

Marcus Agrippa was Octavius's lifelong friend. He was also Octavius's most skilled military leader. Ten years after the Battle of Actium, Agrippa married Octavius's daughter Julia.

Following Agrippa's victory, Octavius landed his army at Epirus, north of the Gulf of Ambracia. Octavius led his troops southward. He camped on a peninsula jutting into the gulf from the north. Antony decided he would fight Octavius at this point. Antony brought his troops to a peninsula on the southern side of the gulf. The two armies faced each other at Actium.

Laying the Trap

Agrippa's navy captured Antony and Cleopatra's second fleet near Corfu. Agrippa then sailed to Actium. He placed his fleet just outside the gulf. Here, he could stop Antony's troops and the Egyptian navy from escaping.

On the mainland, Octavius patiently waited. He knew that Antony's troops still might defeat him in a land battle. So he ordered his troops to stay on the narrow peninsula to the north of Actium.

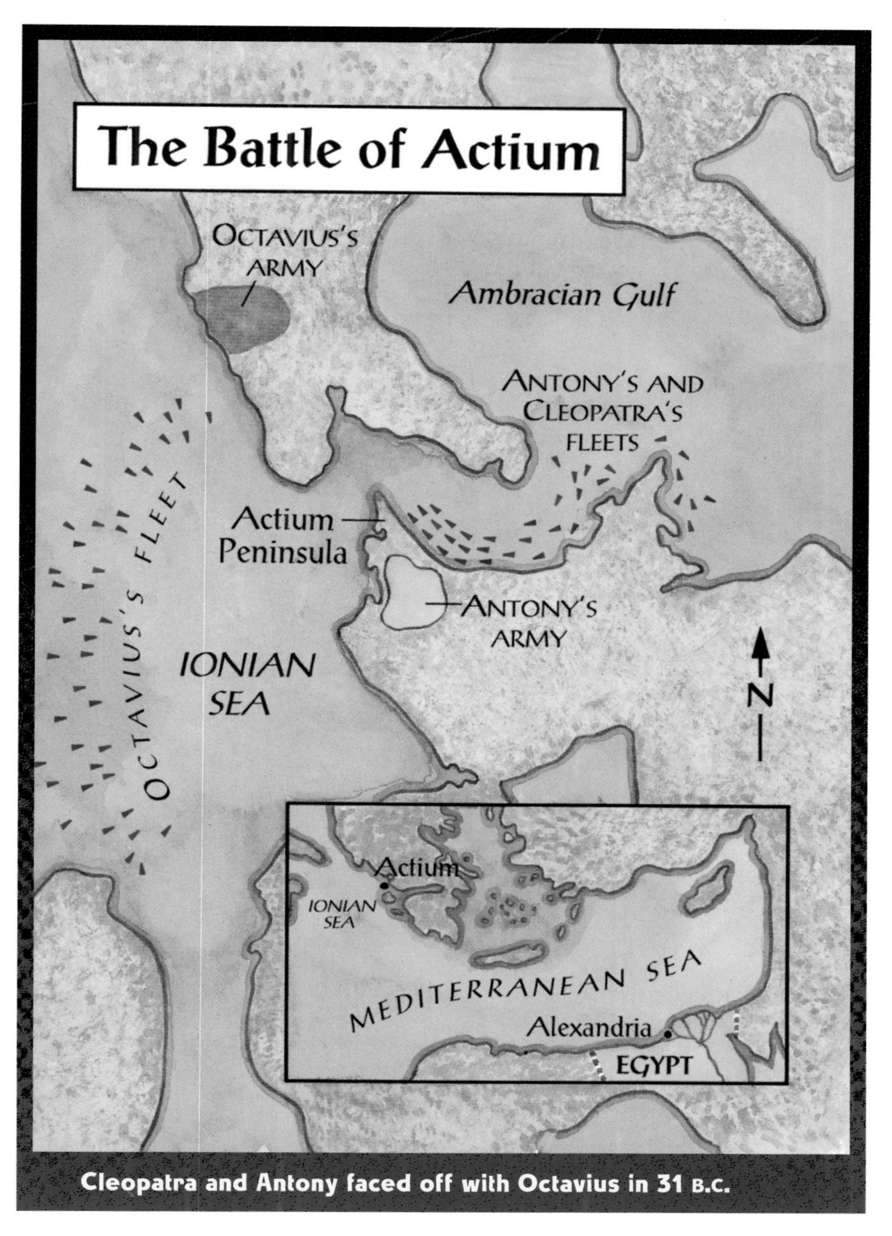

Cleopatra and Antony faced off with Octavius in 31 B.C.

In this spot, Antony wouldn't have room to set up a force large enough to defeat them.

Meanwhile, Antony and Cleopatra were trapped at Actium. With Agrippa's ships cutting them off from Egypt, their supplies were running low. Their soldiers were starving. Many died of malaria and other diseases. Instead of attacking Octavius, Antony thought about escaping. He fought with Cleopatra and his generals. They couldn't agree on a plan.

Cleopatra thought Antony should put their soldiers on the Egyptian ships and attack Agrippa's ships. The soldiers would destroy as many of Agrippa's ships as possible. Then her remaining ships would sail for Rome right away. There, Antony would be able to stop Octavius from returning to the capital. Antony could gather a new army. He could march on Rome to claim the victory.

Canidius Crassus, Antony's second in command, had a different plan. He advised Antony to retreat from Actium. Roman soldiers fought on land, Crassus said, not at sea. Antony should fight Octavius somewhere else in Greece. The best place would be in the open plains. Out in the open,

Antony could stage a large land battle. But this plan would mean the Egyptian fleet would have to fight Agrippa alone. If Agrippa won, he'd destroy the fleet.

Cleopatra was not going to leave her fleet behind. She felt sure that her fleet could defeat the lighter Roman ships. She would destroy Agrippa first. Then she'd have Octavius and his army at her mercy. Going against the wishes of his generals, Antony took Cleopatra's side. He would stay with the queen and fight it out at Actium.

Fighting the Battle

The summer of 31 B.C. wore on. Heat and illness affected troops on both sides. Antony's troops grew hungry and desperate. Many of them went over to Octavius's side. Antony and Cleopatra quarreled violently with their generals and with each other.

In late August, Antony decided on his plan. Instead of trying for victory, he would escape with as many ships as he could. He ordered twenty-two thousand soldiers to prepare to attack Agrippa's fleet. While Agrippa was fighting, Antony and Cleopatra would slip past them to the open sea and freedom. Antony and Cleopatra's crews stored their sails in readiness for the getaway after the fight.

Antony told Crassus to lead the land troops in a retreat to the east after the battle. They were to make their way to Asia Minor. Antony said he would later join them and retreat to Egypt. If Antony and Cleopatra could hold their forces together, they could stop any attack Octavius might later make on Egypt.

A woodcut showing the battle at Actium in September of 31 B.C.

On September 2, Antony and Cleopatra moved toward Agrippa's ships. The two fleets slowly took their positions. Using slings, Antony's men pitched heavy stones at the Roman ships. They threw long javelins across the water toward the enemy soldiers. Ships on both sides used their battering rams to tear holes in the enemy hulls. Whenever two ships approached, soldiers cast hooks to pull the enemy's boat closer. Soldiers leaped across the rails and decks and fought hand to hand with swords, daggers, and spears.

Agrippa's ships were smaller but easier to turn. This ability helped them avoid the larger Egyptian ships. The smaller ships could get in position quicker. They rammed the Egyptian ships over and over again. The long lines of opposing ships scattered. The battle turned into a free-for-all. Meanwhile, Cleopatra held back her own squadron of sixty ships. She watched the action from her flagship. Antony drew Agrippa and his ships slowly to the north, away from Cleopatra's squadron. Her ships slowly rowed away to the west. Suddenly, Cleopatra's ships raised their sails and headed south. They rode the wind into the open sea. Shocking everybody except perhaps Cleopatra, Antony followed his lover.

Ancient Warships

Cleopatra's ships *(below)* were designed to ram and sink enemy vessels. The ships had thick hulls (frames) of wood and iron. Their huge front part, called the prow, was made of heavy bronze. They required large crews and skilled commanders. Octavius's ships were lighter and swifter. They were easier to move around and didn't need large crews. As a result, more of these light boats could be built and used in battle.

At the Battle of Actium, Agrippa had a simple plan. Draw out Antony and Cleopatra's ships. Stay away from their heavy rams. Bombard them with missiles until they're destroyed. Board them and take control. The heavy Egyptian boats couldn't get around quickly. So they couldn't avoid Agrippa's quick fleet. They couldn't get into ramming position either. Agrippa won.

Many historians believe that Antony expected to lose the battle. He had wanted Cleopatra to escape this way. They knew that in this part of Greece, a strong northwest wind often rises in the late afternoon. This wind blows directly toward Egypt. While Antony followed Cleopatra, the rest of his navy fought on into the night. By morning, Antony's ships had either been sunk or had retreated. The next day, the survivors surrendered to Octavius.

Escape to Egypt

Antony and Cleopatra sailed to Egypt. They still had Cleopatra's huge royal treasury. This money would allow them to raise another army and fight another day. But Antony was a broken man. He had lost another battle. Even worse, he had deserted his men.

Crassus marched the rest of Antony's army away from the gulf. Octavius's army soon caught up with Crassus. Instead of attacking, Octavius announced a pardon for Antony's men. He would give them land if they would desert Antony's cause. The army accepted the offer. Crassus escaped to Alexandria to tell Antony.

Octavius, however, could not go to Egypt right away. Many of his soldiers were expecting a reward for their victory. And rebellions were breaking out in Rome. The people of Rome had paid high taxes to help Octavius raise his army. Octavius hurried back to calm the situation. This gave Antony and Cleopatra time to gather new forces in Egypt.

Octavius knew that he couldn't raise any more money by taxing Rome. The only way to pay his soldiers was to conquer Egypt and capture Cleopatra's treasury. Octavius also knew that Antony would soon raise a new army with Cleopatra's help. Octavius could not wait long to act.

Octavius waited until the spring of 30 B.C. By that time, the winter storms in the Mediterranean Sea had passed. He left Rome for Alexandria. He would force another, hopefully final, battle against Antony and Cleopatra.

CHAPTER 8

THE END OF THE PTOLEMIES

THE NEWS OF THE BATTLE of Actium spread. Rulers who had been allies of Cleopatra and Antony switched sides. They saw Octavius as the victor. The leaders of kingdoms in Greece, Asia Minor, and North Africa swore an oath to help Octavius. They realized that if they supported Octavius before the victory, he would reward them when Antony and Cleopatra were defeated. Cleopatra's enemies volunteered to help Octavius. They'd attack Egypt from the east and the west.

The Waiting Game

Antony and Cleopatra could do nothing but wait for Octavius and his forces to arrive. Antony believed his situation was hopeless. He asked Octavius for the chance to live in Alexandria as a private citizen. He agreed to have no rank or Roman privileges. Octavius refused. Depressed, Antony built a small house near the Pharos lighthouse. He lived there alone, away from Cleopatra and his officers.

Cleopatra had her hands full. But she had been in many tough situations before. She sent gifts to Octavius. She asked that he let her live. She asked for Egypt to remain independent. She also asked that Caesarion be allowed to inherit the throne of Egypt.

But Cleopatra wasn't stupid. She put Caesarion out of harm's way. She sent him into the desert near the Red Sea. Cleopatra was determined to fight until she could fight no more. Then she'd flee. She ordered her remaining Egyptian ships to be hauled ashore and dragged across land to the Red Sea. If necessary, she planned to launch them and leave Egypt.

Octavius accepted Cleopatra's gifts. But he refused her pleas. He had no plan of letting Egypt stay independent. Nor was he interested in making Caesarion its ruler. Octavius left Rome in the spring of 30 B.C. He marched into Asia Minor and prepared to attack Egypt that summer.

Meanwhile, Antony knew his defeat was almost certain. He pulled himself together and moved back to the palace. He and Cleopatra again held parties and banquets. He made a final effort to save his territories in the eastern Mediterranean. With a small army, Antony marched out to meet the Romans. He attacked Octavius's troops, at first driving them back. But Octavius's forces quickly regrouped. They forced Antony's army to retreat. Antony sent a messenger to Octavius. He challenged the younger man to hand-to-hand combat to settle their differences. Octavius refused. Antony then tried to bribe Octavius's soldiers to come over to his side. None accepted. Octavius had won.

The day after Octavius's victory, the Egyptian navy in Alexandria surrendered to Octavius without a fight. Some of Antony's soldiers also laid down their arms. Others fled to Alexandria. Meanwhile, soldiers loyal to Octavius marched to the Red Sea. Cleopatra's ships were still at anchor there. The soldiers burned the entire Egyptian fleet. Cleopatra's escape plan also went up in flames.

The Last Days of Cleopatra

The Roman army entered Alexandria. The soldiers surrounded the royal palace. Cleopatra and three of her servants fled. They locked themselves inside a huge mausoleum (aboveground tomb). Cleopatra had prepared this building as her own tomb. Here, she planned to die. Here, she would be buried. She ordered her servants to carry her royal treasury into the mausoleum and hide it in a storeroom.

Meanwhile, Antony received a false message that Cleopatra was already dead. On hearing the news, Antony asked his servant to kill him with a sword. The servant was not willing to commit the deed. He killed himself instead. Antony pulled out another sword and thrust it into his own stomach. He dropped the weapon and staggered to the ground. But he didn't die immediately.

The news of Antony's coming death spread quickly. Cleopatra ordered two servants to bring Antony on a stretcher to the mausoleum. Although

Antony was dying, Cleopatra would not unlock the doors. She feared that Roman soldiers would rush inside and seize her. She ordered her servants to lower ropes from one of the high windows. They raised the stretcher to the window. From there, Antony was gently lowered to the floor of the building. When she saw Antony, Cleopatra began to sob with grief. Antony uttered his final words to her, asking her not to pity him. He gasped his last breath and died.

Octavius entered Alexandria that day. Upon hearing of Antony's death, he immediately sent

Cleopatra holds Mark Antony's body in her arms.

soldiers to the mausoleum. They entered through the same window Antony had used. They captured the queen.

Octavius allowed Cleopatra to go to Antony's funeral. After the ceremony, Octavius said he would take Cleopatra back to Rome as a prisoner. He planned to parade her in his coming triumph. This was the same thing Caesar had done to her half sister, Arsinoë IV. Some disagreement exists about whether Octavius really meant to do this. After all, the Romans hadn't liked seeing Arsinoë paraded. He probably wanted to scare Cleopatra into committing suicide. He asked his guards to leave Cleopatra and her faithful servants alone. He knew that the queen would rather take her own life than suffer any further humiliation.

Octavius was right. Cleopatra bathed, dressed beautifully, and ate a lavish meal. Then she

IT'S A FACT!

Cleopatra is said to have tested various poisons on prisoners. She wanted to know which poisons worked best. None of the poisons worked just right. She next tried animals that had poisonous bites. She finally settled on the asp, an Egyptian snake, for her suicide.

A painting from the 1800s called *The Death of Cleopatra*

carried out a dramatic suicide. No one knows exactly how Cleopatra died. Legend says that she ordered her servants to hide a poisonous snake in a basket of figs. The servants brought the basket past Cleopatra's guards. Cleopatra took the snake from the basket and held it before her. The snake struck Cleopatra. The poison quickly did its work. Her servants also committed suicide. In 30 B.C., Egypt's Ptolemaic dynasty and the reign of thirty-nine-year-old Cleopatra ended.

Cleopatra's Children

For the Romans, even a dead Cleopatra was dangerous. Roman historians loyal to Octavius criticized Cleopatra and her life. They spread tales of Cleopatra's greed. Their reports didn't talk about her successes as queen of Egypt.

No one knows if sixteen-year-old Caesarion made it out of Alexandria. By most accounts, he fled the city. After the death of his mother, his tutor told him that Octavius might pardon him. He would not be allowed to rule over Egypt. But he might be allowed to live. Caesarion returned to Alexandria. But he found out that he'd been betrayed. Octavius had decided to bring Egypt into the Roman Republic. He could not allow such a dangerous rival to remain alive. Caesarion was captured and killed.

The rest of Cleopatra's children were captured and made to walk in Octavius's triumph in Rome. Later, Cleopatra Selene escaped. She managed to go to the North African province of Mauretania (modern Algeria and Morocco). She married King Juba II. Alexander Helios and Ptolemy Philadelphus also fled and survived. But no one knows where they went or how long they lived.

Cleopatra's Effect on the Roman Empire

Later in 30 B.C., Octavius made Egypt a Roman province. He brought Cleopatra's treasury to Rome. The money allowed Octavius to buy land for the soldiers who had served at Actium. Octavius's victory officially changed Rome from a republic into an empire. Strangely, it became a total monarchy, just like Ptolemaic Egypt. Octavius ruled as the first emperor. The Senate gave him the title Augustus (praiseworthy). He became Augustus Caesar.

Octavius ruled the Roman Empire until his death in A.D. 14. He went down in history as the founder of the Roman Empire. Antony and Cleopatra came to be remembered as unlucky lovers and defeated enemies of Rome.

It's a Fact!

The Senate wanted to honor Octavius's victory at the Battle of Actium. The senators gave the name August to the month of the defeat. Octavius built the city of Nicopolis ("Victory City" in Greek) near Actium. He also set up a sports festival known as the Actiaca. It was to be held in Rome every four years. The Actiaca celebrated his victory over the Egyptian queen.

Most people who wrote about Cleopatra's life lived long after the queen's death. Their information came down through many generations. Roman writers changed much of her history to suit their own goals.

Cleopatra, in a traditional Egyptian carving, from the Temple of Hator, in Dendera, Egypt

In fact, Cleopatra had a great effect on Rome. Octavius ruled the Roman Empire in much the same way that the pharaohs ruled Egypt. Cleopatra's realm became an important part of the Roman Empire. The empire needed Egypt's grain and money. Cleopatra remained an important figure in the city of Rome. Her statue remained standing in Rome for three hundred years. Alexandrians and other Egyptians praised her successes. They formed cults that honored her memory.

Cleopatra's Effect on the World

Much later, European painters saw Cleopatra as an excellent subject for their works. William Shakespeare's play *Antony and Cleopatra* (1623) shows Cleopatra as a clever woman who causes trouble. The play portrays Antony as a man who is loyal to his wife but who has a strong passion for Cleopatra. The Irish playwright George Bernard Shaw wrote a witty account of the queen's relationship with Julius Caesar in *Caesar and Cleopatra* (1898). In 1962, Elizabeth Taylor played Cleopatra in a film of the same name. Taylor's Cleopatra was an independent, energetic, and clever woman who had a taste for luxury. She

Elizabeth as Cleopatra

In 1962, Elizabeth Taylor made $50,000 (about $315,000 in today's dollars) a week for acting in the movie *Cleopatra.* According to one writer, she did all she could to match Cleopatra's lavish lifestyle. During the filming, Taylor lived in a large home of pink marble. Every evening, the cigarette holders, matchbooks, candles, flowers, and tablecloths were new. Each matched whatever outfit Taylor was wearing that night. She brought three hundred dresses with her. She threw away each one after wearing it.

happily trapped Mark Antony, who was played by Richard Burton.

In the form of plays, books, and movies, Cleopatra's memory lives on. More than two thousand years after her death, she still keeps people guessing. Some people believe Cleopatra was ruthless and immoral. Others feel she was dedicated and brave. Most agree that this fascinating queen proved herself the equal of any Ptolemaic king in her family. She also stands out as a woman of strength, intelligence, and ambition in what was then a man's world.

GLOSSARY

Alexandrian: a person or thing that comes from the Egyptian port city of Alexandria

ancient Greece: a group of city-states that Macedonia took over in 338 B.C. Rome conquered the area in 146 B.C. and ruled until A.D. 476.

Asia Minor: the territory in southwestern Asia that roughly matches modern Turkey

consul: a person who held a lawmaking position within the ancient Roman Senate

Gabinian: a Roman soldier who served under Gabinius in the last century B.C.

Macedonia: an ancient kingdom that roughly matches modern northern Greece

Mediterranean world: a region that refers to countries or cities close to or on the Mediterranean Sea. This body of water lies between Europe and Africa.

propaganda: false information. Most propaganda hopes to change a point of view about a person or a policy.

Roman citizen: a person born in Rome. To be a citizen of ancient Rome, a person's parents had to be legally married and Roman citizens. Eventually, people in other parts of Italy were granted Roman citizenship. Slaves freed by Roman owners also became Roman citizens. Roman citizens had more rights than other people within the Roman state.

Roman Senate: a group of advisors within the ancient Roman Republic and Roman Empire. To be a senator, a person had to be a male Roman citizen.

triumph: a special parade held in ancient Rome to celebrate a great military victory

Triumvirate: in ancient Rome, a group of three leaders. Each member of the group was called a triumvir. All three leaders were supposed to have the same amount of power. But this didn't always happen.

TIMELINE

The small letters *B.C.* in this timeline stand for "before Christ." They tell us that the event on that date took place before Jesus was born. Events that happened after Jesus' birth start with the small letters *A.D.*

509 B.C. The Roman Republic is set up.

338 B.C. Alexander the Great takes over the city-states of ancient Greece.

332 B.C. Alexander the Great takes over Egypt. While there, he founds the port of Alexandria.

323 B.C. Alexander the Great dies. His generals Antigonus, Seleucis, and Ptolemy divide up his empire. Ptolemy takes Egypt.

305 B.C. Ptolemy names himself Pharaoh (king) Ptolemy I. He founds the Ptolemaic dynasty (family of rulers).

146 B.C. The Roman Republic takes over ancient Greece.

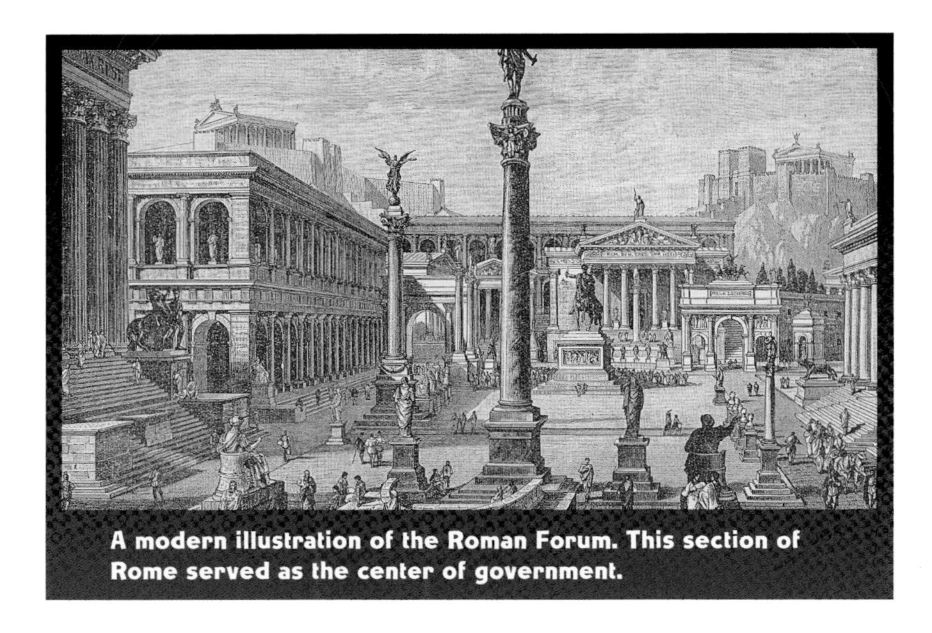

A modern illustration of the Roman Forum. This section of Rome served as the center of government.

80 B.C. Ptolemy XII, nicknamed Auletes (Flute Player), becomes pharaoh of Egypt.

69 B.C. Cleopatra VII is born to Auletes.

60 B.C. Caesar, Pompey, and Crassus set up the First Triumvirate.

59 B.C. Auletes bribes the Roman Republic to stay out of Egypt.

51 B.C. Auletes dies. Cleopatra VII and her half brother Ptolemy XIII become co-rulers of Egypt.

Cleopatra VII

48 B.C. The First Triumvirate ends. Caesar attacks Egypt. Cleopatra flees to Syria. She sneaks back into Egypt and meets Caesar. She wins his support to rule Egypt.

47 B.C. Caesar's troops defeat Ptolemy XIII's army. Ptolemy XIII dies. She becomes co-ruler with her half brother Ptolemy XIV. Cleopatra gives birth to Caesarion, Caesar's son.

46 B.C. Caesar returns to Rome. He invites Cleopatra to visit him there.

45 B.C. Caesar names his great-nephew Octavius as his heir.

44 B.C. Roman senators murder Caesar in the Senate Hall. Cleopatra sails quickly back to Alexandria.

43 B.C. Octavius, Mark Antony, and Lepidus form the Second Triumvirate. The Roman Senate gives Antony control of Roman lands at the eastern end of the Mediterranean Sea.

41 B.C. To show his force, Antony orders Cleopatra to travel to see him in Asia Minor (modern Turkey). He and Cleopatra become lovers.

40 B.C. Antony returns to Rome and marries Octavius's sister, Octavia. Cleopatra gives birth to Antony's twins.

37 B.C. Antony lands in Syria and sends for Cleopatra. He gives her most of Rome's eastern lands.

In this painting of the 1600s, Cleopatra arrives in Tarsus, Asia Minor, to meet the Roman general Mark Antony.

36 B.C. Cleopatra gives birth to Antony's second son.

34 B.C. In Alexandria, Antony names Caesarion, not Octavius, as Caesar's heir. He also gives lands to his three children with Cleopatra. Octavius starts a propaganda campaign to turn Rome against Antony. Antony divorces Octavia.

32 B.C. Octavius declares war on Cleopatra.

31 B.C. Octavius's forces defeat Antony and Cleopatra at the Battle of Actium (in Greece). Both losers survive and flee to Egypt.

30 B.C. Octavius's forces attack Egypt and win. Antony and Cleopatra commit suicide. Egypt becomes a Roman province. Cleopatra's four children flee or are killed.

27 B.C. As Augustus Caesar, Octavius becomes the first emperor of the Roman Empire.

Selected Bibliography

Appian. *Appian's Roman History*, Vol. 4. Cambridge, MA: Harvard University Press, 1955.

Bradford, Ernle. *Cleopatra.* New York: Harcourt Brace Jovanovich, 1972.

Brooks, Polly Schoyer. *Cleopatra: Goddess of Egypt, Enemy of Rome.* New York: Harper Collins, 1995.

Caesar, Julius. *The Alexandrian War.* Cambridge, MA: Harvard University Press, 1955.

Carcopino, Jerome. *Daily Life in Ancient Rome: The People and the City at the Height of the Empire.* New York: Bantam Books, 1971.

Cassius, Dio. *Roman History*, Vol. 5. Cambridge, MA: Harvard University Press, 1955.

Foss, Michael. *The Search for Cleopatra.* New York: Arcade, 1997.

Grant, Michael. *Cleopatra: A Biography.* New York: Simon and Schuster, 1972.

Grant, Michael. *Julius Caesar.* New York: M. Evans & Company, 1992.

Hughes-Hallett, Lucy. *Cleopatra: Histories, Dreams and Distortions.* New York: Harper & Row, 1990.

Josephus, Flavius. *Jewish Antiquities.* Cambridge, MA: Harvard University Press, 1955.

Nardo, Don. *The Importance of Cleopatra.* San Diego: Lucent Books, 1994.

Plutarch. *Lives of the Noble Grecians and Romans.* Translated by John Dryden. New York: Random House, n.d.

Rieland, Randy. "The Search for Cleopatra's Palace," *Discovery Channel Online.* N.d. http://www.discovery .com/indep/newsfeatures/cleopatra/cleopatra (n.d.).

Shakespeare, William. *The Works of William Shakespeare.* The Shakespeare Head Press edition. New York: Oxford University Press, 1938.

Further Reading and Websites

Behnke, Alison. *Italy in Pictures.* Minneapolis: Twenty-First Century Books, 2003.

Bibliotheca Alexandrina
http://www.bibalex.org
The official website of the new Library of Alexandria gives lots of information about the collections, as well as a history of the old library.

Cleopatra on the Web
http://www.isidore-of-seville.com/cleopatra
This site covers many aspects of the study of Cleopatra, from ancient sources to modern movies and DVDs. It has short biographies and discussions of the queen's impact on art through the ages.

Day, Nancy. *Your Travel Guide to Ancient Egypt.* Minneapolis: Twenty-First Century Books, 2001.

Day, Nancy. *Your Travel Guide to Ancient Greece.* Minneapolis: Twenty-First Century Books, 2001.

Foreman, Laura. *Cleopatra's Palace: In Search of a Legend.* New York: Discovery Books, 1999.

History for Kids
http://www.historyforkids.org/learn/egypt/history/romans
The History for Kids site covers places all over the world. The section on Egypt has pictures, biographies, and timelines from ancient times to the present.

Limke, Jeff. *Isis & Osiris: To the Ends of the Earth.* Minneapolis: Graphic Universe, 2007.

Markel, Rita J. *Your Travel Guide to Ancient Rome.* Minneapolis: Twenty-First Century Books, 2004.

McDonald, Fiona. *Cleopatra: The Queen of Kings.* New York: Dorling Kindersley, 2001.

Morgan, Julian. *Cleopatra: Ruling in the Shadow of Rome.* New York: Rosen Publishing, 2003.

Schecter, Vicky Alvear. *Alexander the Great Rocks the World.* Plain City, OH: Darby Creek Publishing, 2006.

Woods, Michael, and Mary B. Woods. *Ancient Warfare: From Clubs to Catapults.* Minneapolis: Twenty-First Century Books, 2000.

Zuehlke, Jeffrey. *Egypt in Pictures.* Minneapolis: Twenty-First Century Books, 2003.

INDEX

Photo Acknowledgments

The images in this book are used with the permission of: © Bettmann/CORBIS, pp. 4, 86; © Laura Westlund/Independent Picture Service, pp. 6, 81; © Bridgeman Art Library, London/SuperStock, p. 8; © Réunion des Musées Nationaux/Art Resource, NY, p. 10; © Getty Images, pp. 11, 15, 76, 79, 100, 104; © North Wind Picture Archives, pp. 12, 51, 84; © Erich Lessing/Art Resource, NY, p. 14; © Stock Montage/SuperStock, pp. 19, 35; University of Minnesota College of Architecture and Landscape Architecture, p. 22; © The Granger Collection, New York, pp. 26, 63, 69, 72, 73, 75, 105; © SuperStock, Inc./SuperStock, pp. 31, 95, 106; © Scala/Art Resource, NY, p. 41; © age fotostock/SuperStock, p. 44; © Mary Evans Picture Library/Douglas Dickins, p. 46; © The Art Archive/Galleria d'Arte Moderna, Rome/Dagli Orti (A), p. 48; © Christie's Images/SuperStock, p. 57; Library of Congress (LC-USZ62-115316), p. 93; © Silvio Fiore/SuperStock, p. 98.
Cover: © Getty Images.